A

Book of
Inspiration

Summersdale Publishers Ltd
46 West Street
Chichester
West Sussex
PO19 1RP
UK

Printed and bound in Great Britain by CPD.

ISBN 1 873475 65 9

Jacket by Java Jive Design, Chichester.

A
Book of
Inspiration

Look well into yourself; there is a
source which will always spring up
if you will search there.

Marcus Antonius

Let us have faith that right makes might; and in that faith let us to the end, dare to do our duty as we understand it.

Abraham Lincoln

Be happy while y'er leevin,
For y'er a lang time deid.

Scottish motto

Know thyself.

Inscribed on the temple of Apollo at Delphi

Quidquid agas, prudenter agas, et respice finem.

(Whatever you do, do cautiously, and look to the end.)

Gesta Romanorum

Resolve to be thyself: and know,
that he who finds himself,
loses his misery.

Matthew Arnold

Mahomet made the people believe that he would call a hill to him, and from the top of it offer prayers for the observers of his law. The people assembled: Mahomet called the hill to come to him again and again; and when the hill stood still, he was never a whit abashed, but said, 'If the hill will not come to Mahomet, Mahomet will go to the hill.'

Francis Bacon

A friend may well be reckoned
the masterpiece of nature.

Ralph Waldo Emerson

With the ancient is wisdom; and
in length of days understanding.

Job. 12:12

Even the woodpecker owes his
success to the fact that he uses his
head and keeps pecking away until he
finishes the job he starts.

Coleman Cox

The voice of him that crieth in the wilderness, Prepare ye the way of the Lord, make straight in the desert a highway for our God. Every valley shall be exalted, and every mountain and hill shall be made low: and the crooked shall be made straight, and the rough places plain: And the glory of the Lord shall be revealed, and all flesh shall see it together: for the mouth of the Lord hath spoken it.

Isiah 40:3

Foresake not an old friend; for
the new is not comparable to him;
a new friend is as new wine;
when it is old, thou shalt drink
it with pleasure.

Ecclesiasticus 9:2

Man is still the most extraordinary computer of all.

J. F. Kennedy

If you have no confidence
in yourself you are twice defeated
in the race of life. With confidence
you have won even before
you have started.

Marcus Gavey

The diamond cannot be polished
without friction, nor the man
perfected without trials.

Chinese proverb

The most important human
endeavour is the striving for morality
in our actions. Our inner balance and
even our very existence depend on it.
Only morality in our actions can give
beauty and dignity to life.

Albert Einstein

What is the use of living, if it be
not to make this world a better
place for those who live in it, after
we are gone.

Winston Churchill

The secret of success is making
your vocation your vacation.

Mark Twain

A man's usefulness depends upon his living up to his ideals in so far as he can. It is hard to fail but it is worse never to have tried to succeed.

Theodore Roosevelt

To laugh often and much; to win the respect of intelligent people and the affection of children; to earn the appreciation of honest critics and endure the betrayal of false friends; to appreciate beauty, to find the best in others; to leave the world a bit better, whether by a healthy child, a garden patch or a redeemed social condition; to know even one life has breathed easier because you have lived. This is to have succeeded.

Ralph Waldo Emerson

Coming together is a beginning;
keeping together is progress;
working together is success.

Henry Ford

Whatever humans have learned
had to be learned as a consequence
only of trial and error experience.
Humans have learned only
through mistakes.

Buckminster Fuller

Nothing in the world can take the place
of perseverance. Talent will not; nothing
is more common than unsuccessful men
with talent. Genius will not;
unrewarded genius is almost a proverb.
Education will not; the world is full of
educated derelicts. Perseverance and
determination alone are omnipotent.

Calvin Coolidge

Man must evolve for all human
conflict a method that rejects
revenge, aggression and retaliation.
The foundation of such a
method is love.

Martin Luther King

Whatever you can do, or dream
you can . . . begin it. Boldness has
genius, power, and magic in it.

W.H. Murray

You and I possess within ourselves,
at every moment of our lives,
under all circumstances,
the power to transform
the quality of our lives.

Werner Erhard

To follow, without halt, one aim:
there's the secret of success.

Anna Pavlova

One person with a belief is equal
to the force of ninety-nine
who have only interests.

John Stewart Mill

Live today like you were going to
die tomorrow, plan for tomorrow
like you were going to live forever.

Thomas Edison

In order to continue to be
winning at the game, you keep
having to play the game.

Ovid

Regret for things we did
can be tempered by time; it is
regret for the things we did not
do that is inconsolable.

Sidney J. Harris

Ask yourself each evening:
What have I contributed today?
What have I learned today?
What have I enjoyed today?

Lucy M. Jachera

Some of my best thoughts are
thoughts of others.

Ralph Waldo Emerson

I have an everyday religion that works for me: Love yourself first and everything falls into line.

Lucille Ball

A wise man will make more opportunities than he finds.

Francis Bacon

Yes, you can be a dreamer and a doer too, if you will remove one word from your vocabulary: impossible.

Robert H. Schuller

You gain strength, courage
and confidence by every experience
in which you really stop to look
fear in the face.

Eleanor Roosevelt

If one advances confidently, in the
direction of his own dreams and
endeavours, to lead the life which he has
imagined, he will meet with a success
unexpected in common hours.

Henry Thoreau

You're about as happy as you
make up your mind to be.

Abraham Lincoln

In order to become the winner that
you will respect and admire . . .
you must have control of the
authorship of your own destiny . . .
the pen that writes your life story
must be held in your own hand.

Irene C. Kassorla

The best years of your life are the
ones in which you decide your
problems are your own. You don't
blame them on your mother, the
ecology or the President. You realize
that you control your own destiny.

Albert Ellis

Be gentle with yourself, learn to love yourself, to forgive yourself, for only as we have the right attitude toward ourselves can we have the right attitude toward others.

Wilfred Peterson

Life is just a mirror, and what
you see out there, you must first
see inside you.

Wally Amos

When you are no longer compelled
by desire or fear . . . when you have
seen the radiance of eternity in all forms
of time . . . when you follow your bliss . . .
doors will open where you would not
have thought there were doors . . . and
the world will step in and help.

Joseph Campbell

How can you come to know yourself?
Never be thinking: always be doing. Try
to do your duty, and you'll know right
away what you amount to. And what is
your duty? Whatever the day calls for.

J. W. von Goethe

Somehow I can't believe that there are any
heights that can't be scaled by a man who
knows the secret of making his dreams come
true. This special secret, it seems to me, can
be summarized in four C's. They are
Curiosity, Confidence, Courage and
Constancy and the greatest of these is
Confidence. When you believe in a thing,
believe in it all the way.

Walt Disney

Self-love is the instrument of our preservation; it resembles the provision for the perpetuity of mankind – it is necessary, it is dear to us, it gives us pleasure, and we must possess it.

Voltaire

No matter who or what made you what you have become, that doesn't release you from the responsibility of making yourself over into what you ought to be.

Ashley Montagu

Self-respect is the noblest garment
with which a man may clothe
himself, the most elevating feeling
with which the mind can be inspired.

Samuel Smiles

Our lives improve only when we
take chances – and the first and most
difficult risk we can take is to be
honest with ourselves.

Walter Anderson

You have the greatest chance of being happy when the voice you respond to is your own voice.

Sonya Friedman

Respect all gods before demigods,
heroes before men, and first among
men your parents; but respect
yourself most.

Pythagoras

There are admirable potentialities
in every human being. Believe in
your strength and your youth.
Learn to repeat endlessly to yourself,
'it all depends on me.'

Andre Gide

Self-respect cannot be hunted. It cannot be purchased. It is never for sale. It cannot be fabricated out of public relations. It comes to us when we are alone, in quiet moments, in quiet places, when we suddenly realise that, knowing the good, we have done it; knowing the beautiful, we have served it; knowing the truth, we have spoken it.

Whitney Griswold

You have everything that is, your thoughts, your life, your dreams come true. You are everything you choose to be. You are as unlimited as the endless universe.

Shad Helmstetter

Love not what you are but what
you may become.

Cervantes

You have to whistle your own tune. You have to walk along the track yourself. Nobody else can lead you. Nobody else can really help you. Once you get the feeling that it is your responsibility, it is the most freeing thing in the world.

Pat Carroll

One often becomes what he believes himself to be. If I keep on saying to myself that I cannot do a certain thing, it is possible that I may end by really becoming incapable of doing it. On the contrary, if I have a belief that I can do it, I shall surely acquire the capacity to do it even if I may not have it at the beginning.

Mahatma Gandhi

A strong positive mental attitude will create more miracles than any wonder drug.

Patricia Neal

In each of us there are places where
we have never gone.
. . . Only by pressing the limits do
you ever find them.

Dr. Joyce Brothers

Everyone should carefully
observe which way his heart
draws him, and then choose that
way with all his strength.

Hasidic saying

Courage means flying in the face of criticism, relying on yourself, being willing to accept and learn from the consequences of all your choices. It means believing enough in yourself and in living your life as you choose so that you cut the strings whose ends other people hold and use to pull you in contrary directions.

Wayne Dyer

Carpe diem quam minimum credula postero.

(Seize the day and put as little trust as you can in the morrow.)

Horace

You are your most important critic.
There is no opinion so vitally important
to your well-being as the opinion you
have of yourself. And the most
important meetings, briefings, and
conversations you'll ever have are the
conversations you have with yourself.

Denis Waitley

Risk-taking is not easy –
and the greatest risk of all is
to try to know oneself, and
to act on that knowledge.

Walter Anderson

Change is the law of life,
those who look only to the past
or the present, are certain to
miss the future.

J. F. Kennedy

Destiny is not a matter of chance,
it is a matter of choice. It is not
a thing to be waited for, it is
a thing to be achieved.

William Jennings Bryant

I hear and I forget. I see and I remember. I do and I understand.

Old Chinese proverb

Discover yourself as a being of light.
Not as an aura but as a pure luminous
consciousness which lights up all things
as it turns towards them. All the rest
(mind-body-spirit) is just the lamp, the
scaffolding, the outside, the wrapping,
the lamp through which God sees.

Pir Vilayat Inayat Kahn

Love is a form of knowledge . . . we
truly know anything or any person,
by becoming one therewith, in love. Thus
love has wisdom that the mind cannot
claim, and by this very hearty love, the
becoming one with what is beyond our
own personal borders, we may take a
long step toward freedom.

The Yoga Sutras of Patanjali

This above all: to thine own self be true
And it must follow, as the night the day,
Thou canst not then be false to any man.

William Shakespeare

Happiness is like a butterfly –
The more you chase it, the more it will
elude you.
But if you turn your attention to other
things,
It comes and softly sits on your shoulder.

Anon

The youth is one who is always astonished and always marvels. He demands, like any insatiable child, 'What next?' He challenges the day and finds joy in the game of life. You stay young, as long as you stay receptive. Receptive to all that is beautiful, good and immense. Receptive to the messages of nature, of man and of infinity.

General MacArthur, 1945

Even the severed branch
Grows again,
and the sunken moon
returns:
wise men who ponder this
are not troubled
in adversity.

Bharthari

It came to me that having life
itself, life being such a miraculous
achievement, is like winning the
grand prize. What we do after –
what we do with our lives – is
the frosting on the cake.

Earl Nightingale

Luck may sometimes help;
Work always helps.
If you do not worry
about a misfortune
for three years,
It will become a Blessing.

Wisdom of The Brahams

We shall not cease from exploration
And the end of all exploring
Will be to arrive where we started
And know the place for the first time.

T. S. Eliot

If you can dream it,
you can do it.

Walt Disney

Don't walk in front of me
For I may not follow.
Don't walk behind me
For I may not lead.
But walk beside me
And be my friend.

Anon

It is only with the heart that one can see rightly, what is essential is invisible to the eye.

Antoine de Saint-Exupery

Far better is it to dare mighty things, to win glorious triumphs, even though chequered by failure, than to take rank with those poor spirits who either enjoy much or suffer much, because they live in the gray twilight that knows not victory or defeat.

Theodore Roosevelt

The harder you fall,
the higher you bounce.

Anon

I keep my ideals, because in spite of everything, I still believe that people are really good at heart.

Anne Frank

Peace is not an absence of war, it is a virtue, a state of mind, a disposition for benevolence, confidence, justice.

Baruch Spinoza

Be patient with everyone, but above all
with yourself. I mean, do not be
disturbed because of your imperfections,
and always rise up bravely before a fall.

St. Francis De Sales

You yourself, as much as
anybody in the entire universe,
deserve your love and affection.

The Buddha

For Mercy has a human heart,
Pity, a human face,
And Love, the human form divine,
And Peace, the human dress.

William Blake

A moment's insight is sometimes
worth a life's experience.

Oliver Wendell Holmes

Believe each day that has dawned
is your last. Some hour to which
you have not been looking
forward will prove lovely.

Horace

It is better to die on your feet
than to live on your knees.

Dolores Ibarruri

Experience is limited, and it is never complete; it is an immense sensibility, a kind of huge spider-web of the finest silken threads suspended in the chamber of consciousness, and catching every air-borne particle in its tissue.

Henry James

The strongest man in the world
is the man who stands alone.

Henrik Ibsen

Let us resolve to build, not to destroy,
and let us remember always
that weakness comes from division,
strength from unity.

Harold Macmillan

It is better to live one day
as a lion than a hundred years
as a sheep.

Italian proverb

Each time a man strikes up an ideal, or acts to improve the lot of others, or strikes out against injustice, he sends forth a tiny ripple of hope, and crossing each other from a million different centres of energy and daring, those ripples build a current that can sweep down the mightiest walls of oppression and resistance.

Robert Kennedy

The soul is placed in the body like a rough diamond, and must be polished, or the lustre of it will never appear.

Daniel Defoe

Man is only truly great when
he acts from his passions.

Benjamin Disraeli

No man is an island, entire of itself; every man is a piece of the continent, a part of the main.

John Donne

Power is given only to him who dares
to stoop and take it . . . one must have
the courage to dare.

Fyodor Dostoevsky

You are free, therefore choose –
that is to say, invent. No rule
of general morality can show
you what you ought to do.

Jean-Paul Satre

Labour to keep alive in your breast that little spark of celestial fire called conscience.

George Washington

Fortune helps those who dare.

Virgil

Patience and longevity
Are worth more than force and rage.

Jean de la Fontaine

Ask, and it shall be given to you;
seek, and ye shall find; knock, and it
shall be opened unto you.

St. Matthew 7:7

Nothing great was ever
achieved without enthusiasm.

Ralph Waldo Emerson

Freedom is not something that
anybody can be given; freedom is
something people take and people are
as free as they want to be.

James Arthur Baldwin

A good laugh is the
best pesticide.

Vladimir Nabokov

If life an empty bubble be,
How sad for those that cannot see
The rainbow in the bubble!

F. Locket Lampson

Happy the man, and happy he alone,
He, who can call today his own,
He who, secure within, can say,
'Tomorrow do thy worst,
for I have lived today.'

Horace

When we can begin to take our
failures non-seriously, it means that we
are ceasing to be afraid of them.
It is of immense importance to
learn to laugh at ourselves.

Katherine Mansfield

Love conquers all things.

Virgil

As you pass from the tender years of youth into harsh and embittered manhood, make sure you take with you on your journey all the human emotions! Don't leave them on the road, for you will not pick them up afterwards!

Nikolai Gogol

Do what you can, with what you
have, where you are.

Theodore Roosevelt

No great thing is created suddenly,
any more than a bunch of grapes or a fig.
If you tell me that you desire a fig, I
answer you that there must be time. Let
it first blossom, then bear fruit, then
ripen.

Epictetus

We ascend to the heights of
contemplation by the steps
of the active life.

Pope St Gregory I

Act well at the moment,
and you have performed
a good action to all eternity.

Johann K. Lavater

To grow old is to pass from
passion to compassion.

Albert Camus

Reflect upon your present blessings,
of which every man has many;
not on your past misfortunes, of
which all men have some.

Charles Dickens

What soap is for the body, tears are for the soul.

Jewish proverb

Love cures people – both the ones who give it and the ones who receive it.

Carl Menninger

If you want to be respected by others the great thing is to respect yourself.

Fyodor Dostoevsky

It is a sign if strength, not weakness, to admit that you don't know all the answers.

John P. Loughrane

You make your own luck. There's something magical in it; I believe that once you've made a decision, some force within you says, 'that is what you want, that is what you're going to get.'

Sir Antony Hopkins

And the little moments,
Humble though they be,
Make the mighty ages
Of eternity.

Julia A. Carney

There is nothing ugly; I never
saw an ugly thing in my life . . .

John Constable

Risk! Risk anything! Care no more for the opinions of others, for those voices. Do the hardest thing on earth for you. Act for yourself.

Katherine Mansfield

One kind word can warm three winter months.

Japanese proverb

Without contraries is no progression.
Attraction and repulsion, reason
and energy, love and hate, are
necessary to human existence.

William Blake

Variety's the very spice of life,
That gives it all its flavour.

William Cowper

The distance is nothing; it is only the first step that is difficult.

Mme du Deffand

Happiness is having a sense of self –
not a feeling of being perfect but of
being good enough and knowing that
you are in the process of growth,
of being, of achieving levels of joy.

Leo F. Buscaglia

Genius is one per cent
inspiration and ninety-nine
per cent perspiration.

Thomas Edison

There is a great deal of unmapped country within us which would have to be taken into account in an explanation of our gusts and storms.

George Eliot

Errors, like straws, upon the surface flow,
He who would search for pearls must
dive below.

John Dryden

It is better to wear out
than to rust out.

Bishop Richard Cumberland

Is it so bad, then, to be misunderstood?
Pythagoras was misunderstood, and
Socrates, and Jesus, and Luther, and
Copernicus, and Galileo, and Newton,
and every pure and wise spirit that took
flesh. To be great is to be misunderstood.

Ralph Waldo Emerson

The glass I drink from is not large, but at least it is my own.

Alfred de Musset

Believe me! The secret of
reaping the greatest fruitfulness
and the greatest enjoyment from
life is to live dangerously!

Nietzsche

We are the music-makers,
We are the dreamers of dreams,
Wandering by lone sea-breakers,
And sitting by desolate streams;-
World-losers and world-forsakers,
On whom the pale moon gleams:
We are the movers and shakers
Of the world for ever, it seems.

Arthur O'Shaughnessy

Sow an act, and you reap a habit.
Sow a habit, and you reap a character.
Sow a character, and you reap a
destiny.

Charles Reade

Small is beautiful.

E. F. Schumacher

There are many wonderful things,
and nothing is more
wonderful than man.

Sophocles

There is no duty we so
much underrate as the
duty of being happy.

Robert Louis Stevenson

That's one small step for man,
one giant leap for mankind.

**Neil Armstrong, 1969
(during the first moonwalk)**

On the whole, human beings
want to be good, but not too good,
and not all the time.

George Orwell

Of all the heavenly gifts that mortal
men commend,
What trusty treasure in the world can
countervail a friend?

Nicholas Grimald

'Tis a lesson you should heed,
Try, try again.
If at first you don't succeed,
Try, try again.

W. E. Hickson

Live all you can; it's a mistake not to.
It doesn't so much matter what
you do in particular, so long as
you have your life. If you haven't
had that what have you had?

Henry James

He is the happiest, be he king or peasant, who finds peace in his home.

J. W. von Goethe

The word which God has written
on the brow of every man is Hope.

Victor Hugo

It has done me good to be
somewhat parched by the sun
and drenched by the rain of life.

Henry Wadsworth Longfellow

The stars are constantly shining,
but often we do not see them
until the dark hours.

Earl Riney

Our own actions are our security,
not others' judgements.

English proverb

A man should never earn his living,
if he earns his life he'll be lovely.

D. H. Lawrence

Everything comes to
him who waits.

Old English Proverb

We arrive at truth, not by reason only, but also by the heart.

Pascal